PAST PERFECT

RICHARD SHAPIRO
HOUSES AND GARDENS

FOREWORD BY
MAYER RUS

EDITED BY
MALLERY ROBERTS MORGAN

PHOTOGRAPHS BY
JASON SCHMIDT

RIZZOLI
NEW YORK

New York · Paris · London · Milan

6.

Foreword

MAYER RUS

10.

Florentine Villa, Los Angeles

132.

Tangier Outlook, Malibu

215.

A Life's Journey

RICHARD SHAPIRO

231.

Master Class

OBJECT LESSONS IN PATINA, FAUX FINISHES, MATERIALS,
AND ARCHITECTURAL DETAILING

FOREWORD | Mayer Rus

RICHARD SHAPIRO IS A FANATIC. THAT WORD MAY CARRY certain derogatory connotations, but its more genteel synonyms—devotee, enthusiast, aficionado—are woefully inadequate in describing the designer's particular passion and monomania. He has a long and varied résumé as a collector, entrepreneur, antiquarian, museum trustee, furniture designer, gardener, and all-around aesthete. But if his life's work had to be distilled into a single obsession, it would surely be the cultivation of the two places he calls home.

The first is a quintessentially Los Angeles, hybridized Mediterranean manor house originally built in the 1920s, which Shapiro has coaxed and caressed into a self-contained world of rare beauty and romance. He calls it the Florentine Villa. The second, a beachfront home on a stunning promontory in Malibu, is a magical folly redolent of Moroccan riads and exotic ports of call. He calls this one the Tangier Outlook.

I won't go into swooning reveries about sublime decorating and fabulous taste here. This book has more than ample images and words that attest to the artistry of Shapiro's creations. More important, this volume is not so much about decorating or taste per se as it is about the quixotic enterprise of crafting a fantasy so persuasive and seamless that even its author must surrender to the illusion.

Don't misunderstand me. There are divine rooms and gorgeous objects aplenty here. Also countless decorating lessons and clever solutions. But there is so much more about the soul of a home, the alchemy of good design, the weight of history, the power of memory, and the recognition that one's abode is ultimately and inevitably an exercise in autobiography.

I've written about houses for nearly a quarter century. Many of them could have been summed up in a paragraph or two describing a series of seemingly random choices meant to signify social status, personality, or some superficial manifestation of one vague style or another. These are places in which the homeowner would be hard pressed to name the artist whose work hangs on the wall, or to discern whether a chair is T.H. Robsjohn-Gibbings or T.J. Maxx. Writing about such empty vessels can be a tough row to hoe.

On the opposite end of the spectrum, there are homes in which every painting, table, and knick-knack tells a story that binds it to the homeowner. These types of houses are deftly imbricated not just with objects but with ideas and narratives that reveal themselves slowly over time. Surprisingly, it's even more difficult to write about such deeply nuanced spaces, specifically because each room and vignette is rife with meaning, inspiration, and the sort of wizardry that defies easy translation into meager words.

Shapiro's homes are exemplars of the latter category—to a degree that few houses ever attain. From their bewitching gardens to their bravura communal and private spaces, every square foot has been considered and manipulated to reinforce Shapiro's illusion of escape from the quotidian realities of time and place. Outside their well-disguised borders, there is noise and smog, commonplace prettiness and unvarnished vulgarity, billboards and traffic lights. Inside, there is serenity, beauty, and wonder.

The joy of compiling this book lies in the opportunity it has afforded to step into Shapiro's world—to share the fantasy, as the old Chanel advertisements used to say. Sitting in the Villa's breathtaking boxwood garden day after day, the initial astonishment at the majesty of the composition and the daring vision underlying it gradually gives way to a more ethereal rapture. There, in that sylvan paradise of artifice and nature, one's spirit is free to soar.

The same can be said of the living room at the Outlook. In that grand, sun-drenched aerie, Roman statuary, ancient architectural fragments, rugged stone floors that echo the footsteps of centuries past, and walls covered in an impasto of antiqued plaster all conspire to cloud the senses. Our eyes, ears, and noses register sea and sky, but exactly which sea and sky? Is it Tangier, Gibraltar, Malaga? We know objectively that the Malibu Country Mart is just up the road, but our hearts are singing *Midnight at the Oasis*.

That kind of experiential legerdemain cannot be conjured easily, regardless of the amount of money applied to the project. The hills and canyons of Los Angeles are overflowing with Tuscan farmhouses, Cotswolds country manors, Loire châteaus, and Spanish alcazars. Most are awful; some manage to rise above the ordinary; and a select few actually honor their architectural forebears in the ingenuity of their conception and execution.

But absolute immersion in a fiction of Old World grace is something else altogether. And this is where Shapiro's fanaticism comes into play. Scraping and gouging wood floors on his hands and knees, endlessly pruning the boxwood to tease out the most sensuous curves, he simply refuses to settle for what most people would consider legitimate verisimilitude. It has taken him years—indeed, a lifetime of study and effort—to create homes that measure up to his noble, nostalgic ideal of cultivated living, and the single-mindedness of his devotion is staggering.

Once again, we return to the dilemma of finding the right words to express sufficiently the transcendent nature of the experiences Shapiro has conjured. If anything, this book attempts to decipher the machinations of his designs while reveling in the sheer delight that those designs engender. Jason Schmidt's brilliant photographs bolster that mission immeasurably. In the hands of a lesser artist, the task of capturing the evanescent beauty and power of these two homes might prove impossible. But filtered through Schmidt's incisive lens, the work truly comes alive.

Of course, Shapiro himself is the true architect of this monograph. Tenaciously obsessing over every aspect of the creative and production process, he has dedicated extraordinary time and effort to create something equal in ambition to the homes he has painstakingly nurtured for decades. And why not? This is his life, and we welcome you to it.

In the dining room, a 1981 Minimalist timber sculpture by Carl Andre is juxtaposed with a sixteenth-century portrait of Saint Peter.

FLORENTINE VILLA, Los Angeles

THE FORGED IRON GATE THAT LEADS TO RICHARD SHAPIRO'S Los Angeles home is nestled discreetly in a monumental, thirty-foot-high hedge of Indian laurel. On the other side of that stately green façade is a self-contained universe entirely out of place and time—the cars disappear; the neighbors disappear; even the city itself seems to vanish in a mist of beauty and grace. Welcome to the Florentine Villa, a Southern California Shangri-La born from the imagination, connoisseurship, and willful alchemy of its creator.

Shapiro fashioned his fantasy of timeworn Tuscan splendor around a Hispano-Moorish house built in the 1920s. The dwelling's generously scaled rooms, period details, and ample garden provided an ideal canvas for the designer to perfect an illusion of Old World gentility and elegance.

From the house's tea-stained stonework to its rusticated floors, no room or surface has escaped Shapiro's obsession with patina. His dogged ministrations have made it nearly impossible to distinguish original architectural elements from those newly added. Within the home's gloriously appointed salons and alcoves, the authentic and the artificial coalesce in a singularly compelling vision of Eurocentric domestic bliss.

Those striking rooms trace the arc of Shapiro's passions and tastes over the past quarter century, encompassing Roman statuary, Old Master drawings, Minimalist sculpture, and Continental antiques of far-flung provenance and pedigree. The designer has marshaled this kaleidoscopic array of art and objects into beguiling ensembles that testify to his mastery of presentation and display—an expertise cultivated over many years of studying great houses and the tastemakers who conceived them.

Shapiro's genius for juxtaposition is announced in the entry foyer, where a first-century Roman torso of an Amazon warrior stands guard before a monumental twenty-first-century target painting. In the dining room, a 1981 Minimalist timber sculpture by Carl Andre gathers strength from its provocative pairing with a sixteenth-century portrait of Saint Peter. Such audacious groupings hint, however deceptively, at a collection amassed over generations by sympathetic polymaths and aesthetes.

The coup de théâtre of Shapiro's exercise in experiential transportation unfolds in the otherworldly garden. There, amid a tapestry of sumptuous, swirling boxwoods inspired by the venerable garden at the Château de Marqueyssac in France, sits what appears to be an authentic neoclassical portico, replete with Ionic columns and a dentilled pediment and cornice. The structure is, in fact, a garden folly, built with redwood and fiberglass meticulously distressed to mimic the gravitas of antiquity.

The pleasure of happening upon the counterfeit temple is hardly diminished by the discovery of the designer's decorative deception. Here, as throughout the property, Shapiro has drawn his magician's cloak over our sense of time and place, and the seduction is complete.

M.R.

The forged iron entrance gate was replicated from an Italian Renaissance design.

Overleaf: A thirty-foot-high Ficus Nitida hedge screens the property from the street. Creeping vines on the façade and roof add to the home's timeworn appeal.

Preceding: Nineteenth-century French stone sphinxes flank the entry to the graveled motor court and the house beyond.

Opposite: The columns, entablature, and rounded pediment are original to the 1920s Hispano-Moorish-style house.

A first-century Roman torso of an Amazon warrior stands guard before a twenty-first-century painting by Gary Lang in the foyer.

Overleaf: A seventeenth-century northern Italian chest of drawers beneath a 1953 painting, fashioned from tissue paper, by German artist Herbert Zangs. A detail of the eroded glaze of a massive eighteenth-century French ceramic garden urn positioned near a heavily carved closet door off the entry.

Preceding: Artworks, furniture, and decorative objects of wide-ranging periods and pedigree converge in the living room.

Opposite: A fourteenth-century Italian sculpture of a bishop.

In a corner of the living room, a Bernd and Hilla Becher typology makes a dramatic counterpoint to a George III console.

Overleaf: A nineteenth-century Napoleon III folding campaign chair beside a crisply tailored white linen sofa. A nineteenth-century Italian scagliola head in front of a mixed-media painting by Otto Piene.

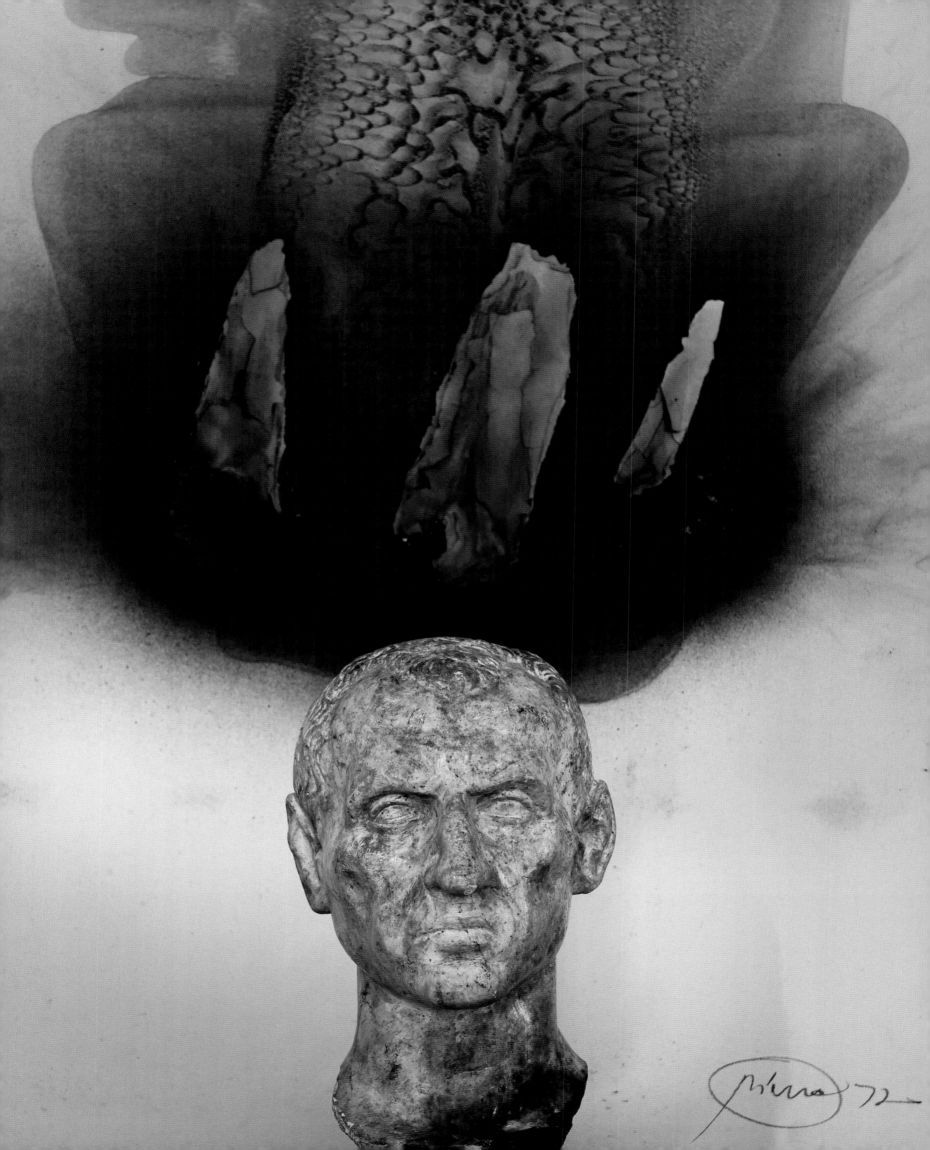

Preceding: Ewerdt Hilgemann's stainless-steel implosion sculpture perches on a stone fireplace mantel. Next to the fireplace, a Bete figure from the Ivory Coast commands the room. At the rear, a seventeenth-century Italian portrait of a cleric hangs on a nineteenth-century French cabinet.

Opposite: A Studiolo antiqued mirror provides the backdrop for a George III console adorned with a group of stone heads ranging from the Hellenistic period through the nineteenth century.

Overleaf: In another corner of the living room, Shapiro fashioned two low tables from tangled roots and fitted them with stone tops. A Henri Michaux ink drawing hangs on a nineteenth-century French cabinet.A detail of a Gutai encaustic painting and collage, circa 1950, by Shozo Shimamoto.

The addition of a decorative pediment strengthens the transition from the living room to an adjacent seating area.

Overleaf: A Piero Fornasetti secretary from the 1950s is flanked by an Anthony Caro steel sculpture on a pine plinth and an eighteenth-century French wing chair in red velvet.

Preceding: Details of the Caro sculpture and Fornasetti secretary.

Left: A Jean-Pierre Khazem photograph rests above a fuchsia lacquer table by Studiolo in the sitting room. An eighteenth-century Venetian torchère and a vintage Josef Hoffmann chair add to the artful mix.

Overleaf: Formerly an alfresco terrace, the enclosed gallery marks the transition from the house to the garden. The Tony Smith piece is joined by a wood sculpture by Joel Shapiro, a sixteenth-century French bench, and a northern European ebonized wood hat rack.

A fourteenth-century French refectory table holds
Roman anatomical fragments and a pair of seventeenth-century Spanish cooking implements.

Overleaf: Bird's-eye view of the boxwood garden.

The rectilinear angles and pale color of a minimalist Studiolo garden bench make a striking counterpoint to the voluptuous swirls of boxwood.

Overleaf: One of the house's original iron balconies from the 1920s informed the design of additional ornamental ironwork, including this curved railing. An eighteenth-century stone religious figure sits at the base of a monumental Ficus Nitida tree.

View from the dining room to the garden. The marble coat of arms is sixteenth-century Florentine.

Overleaf: The dining room is centered on a French Empire table covered in a ruby velvet damask, surrounded by Regency-style chairs slipcovered, unexpectedly, in blue-and-white gingham fabric. A Tatsuo Miyajima LED number sculpture holds one corner of the space.

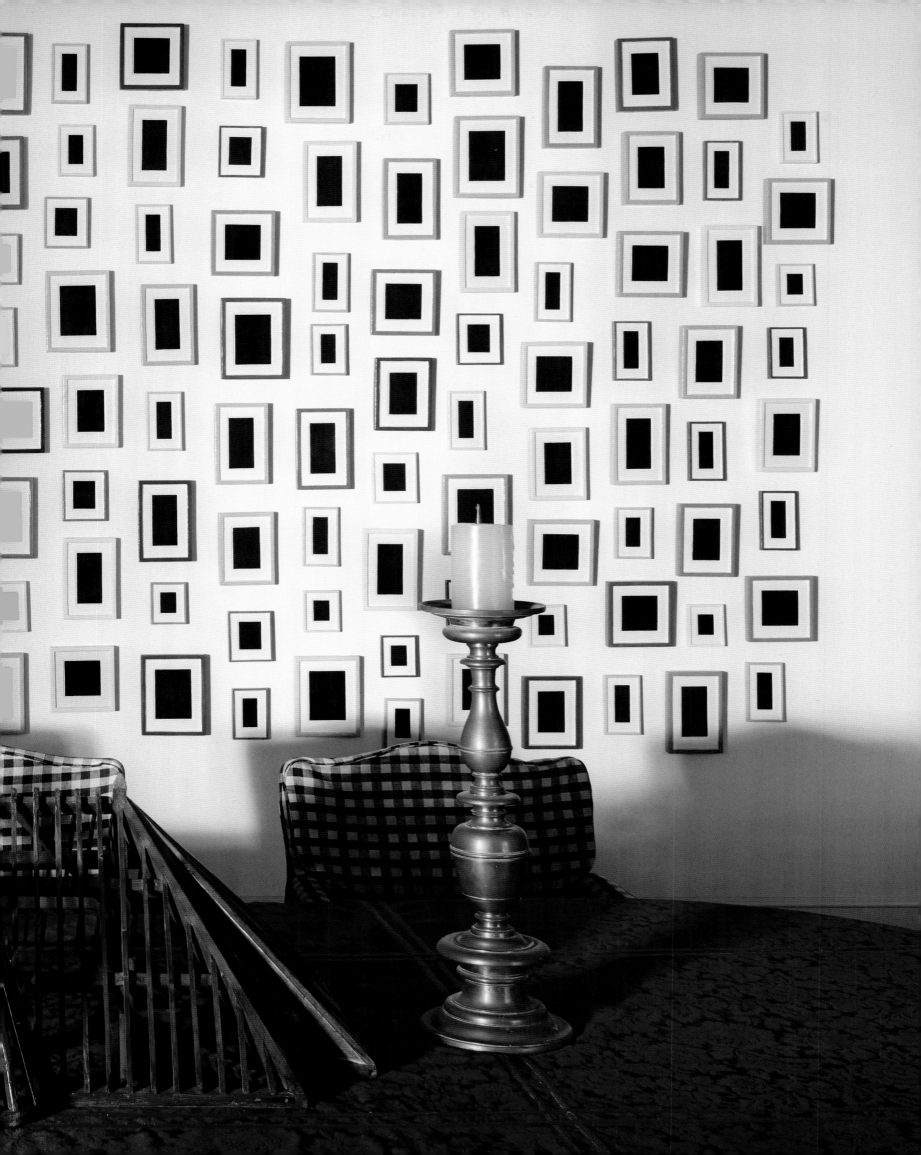

Preceding: A 192-piece installation of artist Allan McCollum's Surrogate *paintings transforms a wall. On the table are a nineteenth-century French architectural model and a pair of seventeenth-century Dutch brass candlesticks.*

Opposite: The gilded mirror and unattributed drawing are both seventeenth-century Italian.

Overleaf: A felt wall piece by Robert Morris faces the Allan McCollum installation across the room; in a niche near the dining room entry, a John Coplans photograph surmounts a contemporary Italian credenza with a grouping of small artworks by Richard Shapiro and a vintage staircase maquette.

The breakfast room is centered on a reproduction burlwood dining table with eighteenth-century giltwood chairs. An antique Japanese root vessel serves as a planter. A terra cotta bust sits on an early-nineteenth-century multicolored marble console table. The sculpture is by Jeanne Silverthorne.

Preceding: Walls covered in green damask contribute to the cloistered ambiance of the library. A 1910 Vienna Secessionist table attributed to Adolf Loos, surrounded by Studiolo upholstered seating, stands on a vividly striped Moroccan carpet.

Opposite: The alcove off the library contains a cast latex sculpture by Robert Overby and a collection of Old Master drawings.

Overleaf: A collection of African masks is laid out on a seventeenth-century Italian table.

Preceding: A mounted coco de mer and small bronze figure on the library mantel. An Ashanti paddle, Baule mask, and Teke figure adorn an eighteenth-century Genoese lacca povera secretary. Above hangs a gouache by Jacques Lipchitz grouped with works on paper by Aristide Maillol, Kurt Schwitters, and Mel Bochner.

Opposite: A seventeenth-century Italian stone bust with a grouping of Old Master drawings.

An eighteenth-century Italian giltwood chair sits beneath a cardboard wall sculpture by Florian Baudrexel.

The upper landing features a diptych by photographer Walter Niedermayr and an image from James Casebere's Monticello *series.*

Overleaf: A nineteenth-century Italian chair alights on a landing in the main stairwell. Above, an eighteenth-century terra cotta Amorino figure sits in front of an ornate seventeenth-century Italian mirror.

A seventeenth-century Italian chandelier hangs from an octagonal soffit in the ceiling of the master bedroom. Ionic columns reinforce the room's classical overtones.

Overleaf: An eighteenth-century Italian giltwood bench in front of floor-to-ceiling bookcases trimmed with picture frame molding.

The bed hangings incorporate textile fragments from an eighteenth-century Indian elephant cover combined with contemporary velvet and metallic tape trim.

A Biedermeier burlwood secretary from 1825 is crowned with a pair of japanned papier mâché urns.

Overleaf: Framed sixteenth-century Italian chasubles (clerical vestments) flank an antique French stone fireplace with a Studiolo iron screen in the master suite's sitting area. On the mantel, a mixed-media artwork by Lawrence Carroll is joined by an array of mementos, including an Indonesian mask and Indian puppets.

The master bath's bronze sink was found in England and retrofitted with Carrara marble. The floor pattern comprises Fior di Pesco and black marbles.

A nineteenth-century French copper and zinc tub occupies a mahogany-framed niche with walls of book-matched marble.

The eighteenth-century duchesse brisée that occupies a corner of the bedroom looks out to a garden folly based on a Palladian portico.

Overleaf: A pair of Romanesque stone lions guards the entry to the pool and garden folly.

The garden folly's design is based on Palladio's drawings for the portico of his Villa Chiericati. Its Ionic columns and pediment, which seem to be made of stone, are in fact redwood and fiberglass, elaborately finished and distressed to mimic antiquity.

Overleaf: A massive antique stone fireplace, found in Antwerp, influenced the shape and scale of the pavilion's interior. Custom curved sofas conform to the shape of the space.

Preceding: Details of the folly. The fireplace is a nineteenth-century copy of a Renaissance original.

Opposite: Genuine architectural fragments bolster the folly's trompe-l'oeil effect.

Overleaf: The swimming pool is bordered in weathered stone, and its interior surface stained a mottled green, to make the modern amenity appear more like a timeworn reflecting pool. The Richard Shapiro sculpture was inspired by the calligraphic strokes of a Brice Marden drawing.

To preserve the insularity of the garden, a passage to a utilitarian side yard is delineated by a studded door set in a neoclassical surround, with vine-covered trellises blocking any visual intrusion.

Overleaf: Encircled by sinuous boxwood, a two-piece dolomite sculpture by Ulrich Rückriem is installed beside a gnarled, hundred-year-old coral tree. On the following spread, a pair of playful eighteenth-century Italian putti frame a view of the back of the house.

Preceding: Richard Shapiro's sculpture resides among a stand of giant timber bamboo.

Left: Detail of a French eighteenth-century stone urn placed in the garden.

Overleaf: A carpet of undulating boxwood spreads out beneath the giant Ficus tree that shelters the outdoor dining area.

An Anthony Caro steel sculpture stands at the base of a small forest of black bamboo.

Overleaf: A system of stepped, concealed terraces made of treated lumber creates a topography of varying elevations for the boxwood display.

Richard Shapiro's monumental steel sculpture rises in a clearing.

Overleaf: Boxwood creates a pillowy surround for a hundred-year-old coral tree.

TANGIER OUTLOOK, Malibu

RICHARD SHAPIRO DREW INSPIRATION FOR HIS SEASIDE home in Malibu from its dramatic site on a promontory overlooking Broad Beach and the azure waters of the Pacific. Unlike the Florentine Villa, the Tangier Outlook, as he calls it, was created from the ground up, on an idyllic plot of land shaded by Monterey cypresses and Schiaparelli-pink bougainvillea—a place that, for Shapiro, instantly conjured visions of a centuries-old Moroccan aerie poised above the Strait of Gibraltar.

To elucidate his dream of exotic Mediterranean ports inhabited by worldly expatriates, Shapiro employed all the skills and sleights-of-hand he had developed for his primary residence in town. The beach house is wrapped in a skin of rusticated plaster, with crawling vines traversing the exterior walls and tiled roof. Inside, the designer revived the archaic technique of lime-and-horsehair plaster, covering the walls in a highly textured finish that simulates the ravages of time and the elements. To bolster that illusion, Shapiro had the walls adorned with Renaissance-style frescoes, which were systematically sanded and eroded to read as pentimenti or vestigial traces of past lives and long ago glories.

The home is entered through a massive seventeenth-century walnut door from northern Italy, which is set in a rounded stair tower. That weighty portal opens onto a soaring, double-height room that encompasses an open arrangement of living, dining, and kitchen spaces. A twenty-foot-high wall of windows and French doors connects the grand interior to the house's upper terrace and the intoxicating seascape that stretches out to the horizon. The master bedroom, perched on a mezzanine above the living area, enjoys the same dazzling view.

At the opposite end of the house, adjacent to a tiled Moroccan courtyard, Shapiro's library is outfitted with mementos of a well-lived and well-traveled life: antique Persian calligraphy, sixteenth-century Syrian tiles, an eighteenth-century Spanish desk, and arched floor-to-ceiling bookcases. A checkerboard floor of worn slate and sandstone tiles, seventeenth-century wood beams from Provence, and walls coated in tadelakt, a traditional Moroccan plaster, complete the heady mise-en-scène.

In the garden, Shapiro planted various types of cacti and aloe along with boxwood, Italian cypresses, fig and orange trees, and climbing pink roses—an enticing mix reminiscent of the Majorelle garden in Marrakech. Whitewashed railroad ties form the parapets, the terraces, and the staircase that descends the steep bluff to the ocean.

Throughout the landscape and the interiors, fragments of classical statuary reinforce the fantasy of a Mediterranean villa bathed in antiquity and cultural cross-pollination. The Pacific Coast Highway may only be a short distance from the house, but thanks to Shapiro's relentless attention to details and nuance, that car-choked thoroughfare might just as well be a million miles away.

M.R.

The Outlook is perched on a dramatic promontory overlooking Broad Beach in Malibu. Landings and alcoves situated on the steep incline offer different vantage points for enjoying the seascape.

Overleaf: A Roman torso stands in the living room. The upper terrace is shaded by a towering Monterey cypress.

The home is entered through a massive seventeenth-century walnut door from northern Italy, which is set in a rounded stair tower.

Overleaf: Architectural details reinforce the fantasy of a Mediterranean villa. The reclaimed antique stone pavers are from Corsica.

View looking back to the street entry. In a nod to the Majorelle garden in Marrakech, the landscape includes various types of cacti and aloe along with boxwood, Italian cypresses, and fig and orange trees.

The front entry surround is built with reclaimed stone from France and crowned with nineteenth-century hand-formed Spanish roof tiles. The iron-studded walnut door is seventeenth-century Italian.

The double-height living room encompasses an open arrangement of sitting, dining, and kitchen spaces.

Crude, non-structural beams and a deeply recessed Moroccan-style window lend character to the stairwell.

Overleaf: The living room is centered on a seventeenth-century Cypriot fireplace. Crisply tailored white sofas contrast with the arabesques of the antique elements.

An African stool provides a bit of decorative chiaroscuro with the taut, white upholstered seating.

Detail of the seventeenth-century Cypriot fireplace. A seventeenth-century Italian mirror hangs above. The power of the décor rests in a limited number of bold gestures.

The sinuous steel staircase to the mezzanine-level master suite is meant to be read as a modern intervention.

A twenty-foot-high wall of windows and French doors connects the grand volume of the living room to the house's upper terrace and the intoxicating seascape that stretches out to the horizon.

Overleaf: The passage to the beach is marked by a Moroccan-inspired landing made of painted railroad ties. On one of the lower terraces, an outdoor chaise is adorned with a cushion made from a tablecloth found in a Nashville thrift shop.

On the following spread, a seventeenth-century Italian Cosmatesque panel of inlaid marble creates a strong graphic element in the open dining area.

Preceding: Looking out to the alfresco dining area, the reed-covered side patio is graced with a mammoth outdoor fireplace. Richard Shapiro created the framed sculpture of blackened timbers.

Opposite: A vintage Moroccan lantern crowns the dining table.

The outdoor dining table is shaded by a canopy made from reclaimed grape stakes. The lantern is Moroccan.

Overleaf: The master bedroom occupies the mezzanine above the kitchen. A glass railing preserves views over the living room to the sea.

A hemispheric niche clad in strategically eroded plaster creates an intimate seating nook near the kitchen.

Overleaf: Dramatic slabs of black basalt form the backsplash and island in the kitchen.

Following pages: Frescoes painted on the walls of the master bedroom were aggressively abraded to disguise their true age.

Preceding: An enormous picture window opens the bedroom to the landscape and sky. The fresco extends to the walls of the main living area.

Opposite: Gnarled beams create a striking foil to the white Thassos marble floor and cubic tub.

Authentic architectural fragments in the garden buoy the illusion of antiquity.

A thickly crenelated, vine-covered wall marks the transition from the front garden to a Moroccan courtyard.

Overleaf: At the far end of the Moroccan courtyard, a Byzantine capital rests on a plaster column between weathered rattan chairs, all enveloped by bougainvillea and cacti. The stairwell leads to the entry of the guest cottage.

Preceding: A Moroccan fountain clad in traditional zellige mosaic tiles rests on a bejmat tile floor arranged in a chevron pattern.

Opposite: Skimmed in blue-gray tadelakt plaster, the library has a checkerboard stone floor and a ceiling of reclaimed beams with a hand-painted chevron pattern in the interstitial spaces. The daybed employs a variety of blue-and-white striped fabrics freely mixed.

Overleaf: A reproduction of a medieval sculpture of St. Michael slaying the dragon rests on the library mantel.

Above the sofa, a densely adorned wall holds an eighteenth-century Spanish mirror, framed Persian calligraphy, vintage photographs, and pottery from Fez.

Overleaf: Beside the seventeenth-century fireplace from Cyprus, a stately antique Spanish desk holds one corner of the library.

Detail of a decorative composition that includes an eighteenth-century Spanish mirror, framed Persian calligraphy, and vintage photos.

Overleaf: Custom bookcases reinforce the house's architectural motifs and rhythms.

Detail of a repaired sixteenth-century Syrian tile, one of many arrayed on a powder room wall.

A hand-painted Moroccan panel is displayed next to the fireplace.

The living room at dusk, with a glorious sunset unfolding.

Overleaf: The oceanfront terrace is lightly decorated with rattan furniture and patterned pillows, deferring to the majestic view.

On the oceanfront terrace, a curved banquette and staircase are constructed from whitewashed railroad ties.

Overleaf: An alcove with a canopy of repurposed grape stakes provides a respite on the way down to the beach.

A LIFE'S JOURNEY | Richard Shapiro

WHAT CAN ONE SAY ABOUT A LOVE AFFAIR, ANY LOVE affair, that spans thirty years? For me, that obsession is trained on my two homes, one in Los Angeles, the other in Malibu. They have never failed to consume me with emotion and desire. I've named them the Florentine Villa and the Tangier Outlook. The first was an existing house that I reworked into a near literal study of a seventeenth-century Tuscan country house. The other, built anew on a bluff's edge in Malibu, was based on the fanciful model of an imaginary, two-hundred-year-old semi-ruin in Tangier, gazing out across the Strait of Gibraltar.

The houses reinvent the ambiance of distant places I love. Both are fictions crafted and composed to allow for the suspension of your awareness of time and place. They are transcendent—imbued with qualities so authentic in appearance, spirit, and mood that their true age and locale cannot be discerned. They are built to deceive, but it is a romantic deception. There, in either house, you really do live in a different and better world.

I have applied my core interests—architecture, design, gardens, and interiors—to these houses. Each is a place apart, a refuge, a sequestered haven, a personal fortress, a cocoon in which I, my friends, and my family enjoy absolute insulation from the outside world. These places contain all that is revered, and at the same time hold at bay all that is not. They are the result of a perfect confluence of desire, imagination, time, and resources, and the reflection of my obsessions with history and distant lands, and with art and period furnishings.

I have scanned my background, looking for the roots of such fixations. A few landmark memories do come to mind. I recall the strange and mysterious odor of oil paint and turpentine from the painting lessons my parents gave me as a child, and how each session at the easel seemed like the beginning of a new adventure. Years later, as an Army private stationed at a base in the Arizona desert, I came upon a small antique store. At first, the shop served as a welcome distraction from the bleakness of military life. It was a quiet hiding place filled with curiosities and cheap carved chocolate-brown reproductions of Renaissance furniture. I found it all very intriguing, and after purchasing a small and unremarkable Persian carpet, I noticed the transformative effect it had on my drab quarters. Although I eschew the term, I began to understand the power of décor.

Most significantly, and for reasons I can't fully explain, I've always been moved by the aura of ancient buildings—particularly their tarnished surfaces, corroded by countless years. Fascinated, I would press my face to age-worn walls from Antwerp to Angkor Wat, trying always to analyze and absorb their antiquity. I would try to breathe in their effect, in the hope that I could reproduce it in America, where the slightest stain on a wall typically calls for a bottle of industrial cleanser or a coat of paint. I aspired to create an authentic Old World environment, one so convincing that a sophisticated visitor would forget where he was upon passing through my gate and into my home.

Being a good copier, however, is not a simple matter. First, you need to see and clearly understand the essence of what is to be duplicated. What is its scale and exact shape? Is it cracked, split, warped? Does it have rust, moss, pitting? Are the color and patina mottled with age? To copy well, techniques must be developed to achieve such effects. My homes are the distillation of years of dogged and microscopic study and observation of not only architecture, gardens, and interiors, but most particularly the pursuit of this process of self deception.

This was not about interior design or decoration. It is deeper and more spiritual—a shift to a place where neither the curtains nor the tables and chairs are particularly important, but rather the impression that one has been removed to new and magical surroundings. It's an exercise that requires much intricate and painstaking work, but the result appears to have been effortlessly achieved, even inevitable.

Interestingly, the first application of my imitative skills and methods was focused not on a home, but rather a restaurant, the Grill on the Alley in Beverly Hills, which I designed and co-founded in 1984. My concept was the "watering hole as refuge," a "joint" in the mold of the iconic American brasseries found in major urban centers across the country. Great food being a given, the key ingredients would be atmosphere and theatricality. My guiding lights were lively and venerable eating establishments such as the Brooklyn steakhouse Peter Luger; Bookbinder's in Philadelphia; the Hollywood chophouse Musso & Frank; Tadich Grill in San Francisco; and—my favorite—Kronenhalle in Zurich. Naturally, I hoped the Grill would one day take its place alongside these bastions of Old World food and service.

I studied them carefully. I was even thrown out of one when a manager caught me measuring the banquettes and the width of the aisles. I appointed the Grill with leather booths, their steeple-like posts terminating in bronze coat hooks; black and white marble floors; tall, molded, and coffered ceilings; globed chandeliers; and lots of mirror. The walls were lined with the hundreds of framed drawings I would unearth and hang over many years. The Grill on the Alley would in fact go on to legendary status, playing host to the who's who of Hollywood, captains of industry, and movers and shakers of every stripe.

Detail of an eighteenth-century French wing chair and a Piero Fornasetti secretary in a sitting room off the main living room.

For me, travel was always the best classroom. As I became increasingly serious about my fields of interest—and the seed of an idea for planning and building my own houses took root—I made dozens of trips to Europe, visiting galleries, dealers, and collectors. I never missed a Venice Biennale, a Parma antique fair, a Biennale des Antiquaires in Paris, or an installment of Art Basel. As their counterparts appeared in the United States, I attended those as well. I can't overstate the rush I felt during these sojourns—the sense of anticipation when pursuing a particular piece, or simply the thrill of never knowing what might be waiting for me around the next corner. The adrenaline was always at open throttle.

But I learned to take a calmer view. As my interests coalesced, I began to meet many accomplished dealers, collectors, and curators—people who had spent their lives steeped in history and high culture. I was fascinated by their attitudes toward design and collecting and, indeed, their very way of life. Some were specialists who focused exclusively on one field, such as primitive art or the antiseptic minimalism of Donald Judd and Carl Andre. Their homes ranged from severe and sterile lofts to elegant urban townhouses dripping with anything that spoke to the tastes and sensibilities of their owners. These collectors were true connoisseurs. Not only did they each have a unique point of view, they also had the knowledge and discipline to seek out the best while never succumbing to the obvious trophies on the covers of auction catalogues. They were concerned not particularly with beauty and preciousness, but more with the history of an artwork and its place in the continuum.

I vividly recall a visit to the Berlin home of one giant of the art world, who collected the work of just four twentieth-century artists, the only ones he thought mattered: Andy Warhol, Cy Twombly, Robert Rauschenberg, and Joseph Beuys. Throughout the house, artworks by that estimable quartet were juxtaposed with Roman antiquities displayed on plinths made of raw, knotty pine. I would later appropriate this simple technique for my own collection.

View of Palladio's Villa Chiericati; the Bay of Tangier, opposite.

I was always taken by collections housed in surprising and unusual surroundings: a reworked barn, a shabby stone house, a converted church, or an industrial space. I loved seeing rigorous modern art played off against frescoed walls, warped wooden beams, and worn stone floors. From these exemplars I came to understand the importance of context and placement; how to create a dialogue both among works of art and between them and their environment.

I was a good student, not above sitting at the feet of those from whom I could learn. I developed an instinct for what constitutes intelligent collecting and true connoisseurship. Because I am blessed with a near-photographic memory—you always remember what you love—I realized that I had a repository of thoughts, images, surfaces, objects, vignettes, moods, and nuances, all of them absorbed from travel, observation, and analysis. They were simply mopped up and filed away in what I call my mental archive. Drawing on this resource, I formulated rules, strategies, and principles that guided my own collecting and the way I would create my homes—two places of refuge where

I could pursue a fantasy of living elsewhere, while of course remaining put.

Abetting this effort was my tenure for several years as a trustee at the Museum of Contemporary Art in Los Angeles. When it comes to such institutions, my favorites are always the small and intimate venues like the Abteiberg Musuem in Mönchengladbach, Germany, and the Dia Art Foundation in New York.

The house that I now call the Florentine Villa, built in the 1920s, was itself a fantasy of sorts: Hispano-Moorish, not truly a mansion but the kind of tastefully exotic architectural confection that designers such as Wallace Neff or Addison Mizner devised for grandees of the silent-movie era. It was a nod to another time and place, but that was merely a stylistic gesture. My objective was much more ambitious and comprehensive. I sought to create not merely an Italian-inspired house, but one where every detail and nuance would be as close to authentic as possible and would abet the deception that, within its confines, you were truly in the Tuscan countryside.

While embracing this compulsion—there's no

other word for it—I realized that I had two goals: artifice and artfulness. I wanted to create the illusion of another place, yet within that illusion there had to be an actuality of grace and intelligence. There would be essential aspects to my design of the Florentine Villa that would serve both ends and prove invaluable later, when I created a home drawn from an imagined windswept clifftop in Tangier.

The first fundamental was seclusion: that the property be so visually screened that when one is either on or off the premises, there is no sense of what lies beyond. The deception starts on arrival. A visitor passes through forged iron gates—copied from those at Villa San Michele, a fifteenth-century estate (now a hotel) on a hilltop outside Florence—flanked by a pair of nineteenth-century stone sphinxes I found in a Nice antique shop. The margins of the grounds have been planted with thirty-foot-tall stands of dense Ficus Nitida, as well as Japanese timber bamboo. Creeping vines cover the perimeter walls, as well as those of the house.

Any surface, architectural element, or detail that is meant to be perceived as aged must have the proper scale, fabrication, aging, patina, and texture. The Florentine Villa's exterior was obsessively coaxed into antiquity. I stained (not painted) the walls an ochre color that, with the sheath of vines, gives the house a worn and mysterious aura. The stonework around the stucco walls was darkened with repeated doses of tea and coffee, and pea gravel covers the walkways. My passion for patina found its most elaborate expression in a garden folly that sits at the end of the

A timber sculpture by Richard Shapiro rises in a dense copse of boxwood and bamboo along a garden path.

swimming pool. It is a small-scale iteration of Palladio's portico at the Villa Chiericati near Vicenza—one of the most beautifully proportioned classical buildings in all of Italy. I consulted the construction drawings in my copy of the sixteenth-century architect's *Four Books of Architecture*. My version was constructed of redwood and fiberglass—not the most glorious of materials, admittedly—which were then distressed, degraded, abraded, chipped, and sanded.

With the help of a Hollywood set decorator, the edifice was patinated with plaster, lime, and an appropriately mottled pigmentation that simulates the appearance of weathered ancient stone. The result is so effective that I tell gullible visitors that it is an actual Roman ruin I had shipped to America. To complete the illusion, I reworked the swimming pool with worn stone and stained its surface a mottled moss color, giving the water a murky and brackish appearance reminiscent of the carp-stocked ornamental pond at the Palazzo del Te in Mantua. At night, the reflection of the portico in the still, green water adds a perfect and convincing note to this conjured tableau of noble decrepitude.

Each room in a house should say something, I believe, and particular rooms should say particular things. The interior spaces of the Florentine Villa manifest in one way or another the effects that I see as the fundamental elements of a unique sense of place—the identity that transforms a building into a home. I'll start with the foyer. The entry of a home must be warm and welcoming, but it should also make an announcement. It is a visual and sensual overture that hints at what a visitor will discover in the house.

The Florentine Villa's foyer has an original twenty-foot coffered mahogany ceiling. It opens onto a stairway with an unusual forged iron railing, also original, with swirling arabesque balusters. In the stairwell stands a broken artifact of antiquity—a first-century Roman marble torso of an Amazon warrior—and nearby is a seventeenth-century Northern Italian chest of drawers. A vivid target painting by Gary Lang hangs above the first stair landing. It's a powerful ensemble of mixed materials—stone, metal, wood—that incorporates two millennia of art and design. The effect on newcomers is slightly dizzying, as it is meant to be, and instantly announces the sort of mix that will be found throughout the house.

From invaluable time spent with those I considered genuine scholars and authorities, I learned that the central pillar of effective presentation of art and design is juxtaposition. Great works draw strength from one another, either by their contrasts or by their dialogue with one another. I can vividly recall a visit with the late Swiss art dealer Thomas Ammann, whose Zurich home featured stunning art deco furniture, paired on that occasion with a cache of Roy Lichtenstein paintings. The furnishings—with their modernized neoclassical lines and glowing lacquer surfaces—and the Lichtensteins, with their bright Pop interpretations of timeless themes, seemed like two generations of the same family, their jaw-dropping quality being the common linkage.

Such juxtaposition is the heart and keystone of the Florentine Villa's drawing room design. To enhance the room's architectural forces, I installed soaring, arched Palladian-style windows set with panes of wavy salvaged glass, as well as wide, elaborately carved ceiling trim moldings. The room is a cluttered collector's space, representing a wide range of interests. Following my usual brief, there is nothing here that is simply pretty or decorative. A life-size fourteenth-century carved wood Italian sculpture of a bishop rests atop a pine plinth (again I bow to the Berlin collector's method) facing a stainless-steel "implosion" sculpture by the German artist Ewerdt Hilgemann sitting on the stone fireplace surround. Nearby, two bronze Moroccan urns have been placed on an eighteenth-century Chinese lacquer table.

The artworks on the walls include a small seventeenth-century Italian portrait, a large collage by the Gutai master Shozo Shimamoto, and a nine-piece typology depicting water tanks, made by the German photographers Bernd and Hilla Becher. Flanking a passageway to another room are two gilded George III consoles, one of which supports a grouping of busts that range from the Hellenistic period to sixteenth-century Italian to French Gothic. As these pieces speak to one another, they also speak of my evolution as a collector and designer. This is a laboratory in which I have worked through many curatorial experiments—some succeeded, others failed. But most important, it is a room to which I and my friends can always return and find something new to see: a never-noticed affinity; a suddenly striking contrast; or the spark for a long-lost memory. It is a living room.

My dining room, conversely, is a more formal, relatively austere space. It was built as a new addition to the house some twenty years ago, and its style and proportions—closely spaced, unpainted beams; dentil cornice moldings—were modeled on those of a room

Anchored by a Tony Smith sculpture, the colonnaded gallery strikes an amicable accord between the classical and the contemporary.

in a Venetian palazzo. As well as a place for meals with friends and family, it is meant for the display of art. The antique French Empire dining table sits between two long walls that feature a large Robert Morris felt hanging sculpture facing a 192-element installation of works from Allan McCollum's *Surrogates* series. In one corner hangs a sixteenth-century Old Master portrait of St. Peter, who gazes down on a 1981 minimalist timber sculpture by Carl Andre. Through tall French doors, one views the swirling forms of the boxwood garden and a massive, sculptural Ficus tree. In fact, the garden is so striking that I'm told it constitutes a distraction from the house's interiors.

We think of the rooms in houses as being either public spaces—those designed with visitors in mind—or private spaces, reserved for the owners and their family alone. I don't much care for such hard-and-fast distinctions, but I do feel that rooms should express the personalities, tastes, and collecting interests of their owners. They all should also be suitably comfortable and encourage frequent use. Two rooms in the Florentine Villa do that particularly well. One is my library, which

I used to call the Gun Room, in reference to a collection of eighteenth-century flintlock rifles from the French and Indian War that I, a history buff, once kept there. I later sold the rifles to help finance the purchase of a Frank Stella painting. Now, some thirty years later, the library has been reinvented as a sensuous jewel box of a room, its walls sheathed in green damask.

That fabric gives the room more intimacy and makes for a gentle environment in which I have hung delicate works on paper by Aristide Maillol, Jacques Lipchitz, and Kurt Schwitters; a photograph by John Coplans; and an array of Old Master drawings. On a seventeenth-century Italian octagonal table I keep a collection of African masks, which are illuminated by a cast bronze lamp by Patricia Roach. The mix also includes a seventeenth-century Genoese secretary decorated in lacca povera (which translates literally as "poor man's lacquer" but is really decoupage); a large architectural model of an Italian cathedral; and a Vienna Secession table by Adolf Loos resting on a vividly striped antique Moroccan rug.

My bookish bedroom is similar in spirit. It

was built fifteen years ago, configured from a warren of smaller rooms and painted entirely with flat white water paint. But I made a concerted effort to give the space a deeper patina of age. The ceiling boasts a dramatic, heavily molded octagonal recess, from which hangs an eighteenth-century bronze Venetian chandelier. Bookcases stand the height of the room. Their compartments are bordered with gilded and distressed picture-frame molding based on a Jacques Garcia design. The floor is made of oak boards in a chevron pattern, which I painstakingly (and obsessively) distressed with a hammer and chisel, making sure that each board was separated precisely by the thickness of a credit card to simulate shrinkage. The floor is finished only with a lovely, mellow tinted wax.

The bed has a canopy made from the cover of an eighteenth-century Indian howdah—the tented carriage set on an elephant's back—that I found in a dirt-floored shop in Jaipur and cut into panels. In my mind, it is the sort of prize that a European merchant or soldier might have carried home from Asia. The mahogany and mirrored bathroom's antique copper tub occupies a

niche sheathed in striking, book-matched Fior di Pesco marble. The room appears as though it was plucked from Claridge's in London or the Grand Hotel in Florence. This kind of reverie is what these most personal rooms—my library and my bedroom—inspire. They are transporting places.

As I look from the bedroom windows, the enormous expanse of pillowy boxwood and carefully laced trees jolts me to attention. I created this meticulous landscape as the result of a chance visit to the Château de Marqueyssac in southwestern France. To this day, I am the only person to shape these plants, following a sculptural process no different than if the medium was stone or wood. Punctuating this canvas are Italian cypresses, bamboo, and palms; there are also fragmentary antiquities—columns, capitals, and the like—as well as several large-scale sculptures of my own creation, ranging in material from steel to massive timbers. At the window, I often settle in a chair, actually a duchesse

Detail of the garden at the Château de Marqueyssac; opposite, ancient wall in Bab el Assa, Algeria.

brisée, to ponder, dream, and muse, all at a safe distance from the real world.

As all my efforts at the Villa came to fruition, I found myself, perhaps unconsciously, open to the idea of another major project. Almost a decade ago, I discovered an idyllic oceanfront bluff in Malibu. With only a roofless surf shack, the aerie had a magnificent panoramic view of the Pacific Ocean. Its majesty took my breath away. As I listened to the crashing waves, I suddenly had a vision that I was an American expat, starting a new life in a house on a rocky outcrop in Tangier, gazing across the Strait of Gibraltar to the Spanish coast. I could visualize every detail of the structure: centuries-old, often-repaired whitewashed walls, crooked tiles, a garden with an improbable combination of citrus, bougainvillea, palms, and cacti.

Associative memories flooded my mind: the secretive riads, those traditional Moroccan houses with interior courtyards; ancient fortresses; pigmented plaster walls; ornate inlaid furniture; Berber rugs. I thought of the artists who had come to Tangier seeking escape and exoticism, from Paul and Jane Bowles to interior designer Bill Willis and his dazzling Arabian confections to Yves Saint Laurent and the enchanting Villa Mabrouka.

So for the second time I decided to make an imagined refuge a reality. That very day I sketched my ideas for the future structure on a piece of paper; the configuration would essentially never change. All the knowledge I gained and the methods I mastered while

The view from the kitchen sink looks to a Richard Shapiro timber sculpture tucked discreetly in a side yard.

realizing the Florentine Villa would apply here. This would be the project for which I had been in training all my life. Only the ethos would change, this time borrowing from all that I loved about Morocco—bits of Marrakech, Fez, Essaouria, and the villages of the High Atlas.

The site was atypical for Malibu. It wasn't tucked into an endless row of side-by side homes less than five feet apart—after all, one cannot discover a centuries-old ruin within sight of a faux Cape Cod or a midcentury post and beam. Instead, rising in a grove of Monterey cypress trees, some as old as 250 years, the house could enjoy total seclusion and privacy, but with intoxicating sea views. I designed the place to look as if it had been occupied by various owners over generations. The new plaster exterior was intentionally soiled, broken, and cracked, and the repairs left obvious, simulating the surfaces of their ancient European forebears. I trained vines to grow on the walls and up onto the roof, which was made of imported nineteenth-century hand-formed tiles. The exterior terraces and patios were paved with rugged stone salvaged in Corsica.

Inside this seemingly rescued shell is a minimal interior blending old with new. The centerpiece of the house is a double-height, timber-beamed living room boasting twenty-foot-high windows with the narrowest of steel frames—installed, in my fantasy, sometime in the 1800s—looking out to the sea. Anchored by severe, boxy, white linen upholstery, the space's decorative highlight is a seventeenth-century carved stone fireplace from Cyprus. The surprising height and volume of the room work a trick on visitors, suggesting a much larger structure than actually exists.

The interior walls are sheathed in lime-and-horsehair plaster, a technique born in the Renaissance. The surfaces are made to look old and oft mended, with barely visible vestiges of once vibrant ancient frescoes. The floors were fabricated from two-inch-thick stone slabs, cut in squares, ground down at the edges, and laid without grout. The stairway to the second floor was fitted with a sleek, undulating steel balustrade meant to be construed as an obvious contemporary insertion. It succeeds equally as both a sculptural and functional element. The contiguous open kitchen consists of large, monolithic, basalt-clad blocks concealing cabinetry and appliances, all very much inspired by the muscular work of Richard Serra and Tony Smith.

At the opposite end of the house is the library, its walls done in dark gray-blue tadelakt, the traditional Moroccan plaster. The room has a crude checkerboard stone floor of worn slate and sandstone. The floor-to-ceiling bookcases with arched recesses were inspired by Moroccan designs, and the hand-painted ceiling is crisscrossed by twisted seventeenth-century beams I brought from Provence. Framed sheets of antique Persian calligraphy, vintage Middle Eastern photography, displays of Fez pottery, and a collection of sixteenth-century Syrian tiles line the walls.

In a nod to the Majorelle garden in Marrakech, I planted many types of cacti and aloe along with box, rosemary, fig, orange, Italian cypress, and climbing pink roses. It's a strange and exotic mix that suggests the hands of many idiosyncratic gardeners at work across the decades. I frequently walk from the house, rubbing a hand over its rough walls, and into the garden, smelling the fragrance of the flowers and herbs, and then to the edge of the bluff and the fantasized view of the Mediterranean and the Rif encircling Tangier. From there I descend a rugged curved staircase through a fortresslike portal to the sandy beach below; in this passage there is a sort of magic.

I have devoted the best part of three decades to conceiving and realizing the Florentine Villa and the Tangier Outlook, and I frequently ask myself if the mission has been a success. Have these personal enclaves lived up to my hopes and dreams? Have I sufficiently deceived myself and been transported to other times and places? As I now stroll through the grounds, can I truly feel the wonder of what I've fashioned?

The answer is a resounding "Yes," but there are caveats. The real world, it turns out, has a way of intruding. And I suppose I will always measure my creations against the genuine articles I know so well, and wonder if mine are in some ways false or lacking. But my romantic spirit always manages to push such troublesome thoughts aside.

When I'm alone and left to my own musings, I am deeply submerged in the ambiance I have created and I feel myself falling completely for the ruse I have perpetrated. I wander through the rooms and gardens, letting the effect wash over me, recalling in archaeologic fashion the myriad experiences and exposures, one at a time and cumulatively, that have brought me to this place. Upon awakening each day, coffee in hand, I reflexively wade out into the boxwood garden or walk to the edge of the bluff. In each case, the effect is the same, almost startling, even surprising. And I fall in love with these places all over again.

Snow Pole cacti paired with an Italian seventeenth-century stone capital in the Outlook garden.

MASTER CLASS

*Object lessons in patina, faux finishes,
materials, and architectural detailing*
R.S.

*Detail of an eighteenth-century Italian giltwood chair on a wood
floor painted with a trompe l'oeil inlaid marble pattern*

ANTIQUITY, REAL AND IMAGINED

Placing authentic antique stone elements—columns, capitals, and various fragments—alongside faux versions can result in a very convincing blend. Situated at the end of the pool is my reproduction of the portico of Palladio's Villa Chiericati, which I copied from a book containing the sixteenth-century architect's actual plans. The newly created columns were made of redwood and fiberglass, heavily gouged and eroded with chisels and electric grinders, and then coated with multiple layers of a lime mixture in various hues—all in the service of simulating the patina of age. I placed genuine Roman fragments alongside the new columns to bolster the trompe-l'oeil effect. The vines that envelop the structure further enhance the mood. The fireplace, a nineteenth-century copy of a Renaissance original, influenced the shape and scale of the pavilion's interior space. I bordered the swimming pool with old, weathered stone. The interior surface was re-plastered and stained a mottled green, giving the water a brackish appearance that makes it look more like a reflecting pool. I placed other Roman fragments in strategic spots throughout the garden to reinforce the antique ambience. This strategy was duplicated at the Outlook (overleaf), where I used a pair of seventeenth-century slate staircase panels, a Venetian capital fragment, and a weathered nineteenth-century column shaft to lend gravitas to a side patio.

ORNAMENTAL IRON

Ornamental metal gates, window grates, balustrades, and railings should have the heft and appearance of authentic wrought iron. Cheap-looking tubular material never looks as good as solid stock. In terms of scale, it's best to err on the large side—an extra eighth- or quarter-inch of thickness can make all the difference in the ultimate effect.

The complexity of the design should be appropriate for its application. At the Villa, an original iron balcony on the façade of the house (opposite) set the tone for my own designs. I based the entry gate (right) on an archival Tuscan design. The quality of the gate's fabrication was well worth the effort and expense—after all, the entry introduces visitors to the experience I've crafted.

When it comes to color, I often eschew dark black in favor of softer shades of gray, putty, or white, as I did on the balconies at the Outlook (right, below).

BOXWOOD

The elaborate boxwood garden was inspired by a chance visit to the Château de Marqueyssac in the Dordogne region of France. In laying out the garden, I developed a system of stepped and concealed terraces made of treated lumber to create a topography of varying elevations, despite the perfectly level underlying terrain. Large, mature boxwood plants, usually ten or more years old, were trucked from a farm in Oregon. Prior to planting, I delineated the position of the boxwood and the intersecting gravel paths directly on the ground using chalk, based on my own visual judgment. After their installation, I hand-sheared the wild, bushy plants, either individually or in combinations, into the desired forms. This sculptural exercise is no different than if the medium was wood or stone.

WALLS AND DECORATIVE PLASTER

With the exception of the library, all the interior walls in the Outlook were done in unpainted lime and horsehair plaster, with bits of the hair clearly visible. The surface was variously troweled to simulate the ravages of time and many repairs. Along the beamed ceiling line are vestiges of frescoes I commissioned, which were initially vivid but then sanded away to leave only faint traces. In the master bedroom (above), the headboard is an exercise in shape rather than pattern or color. I kept it white to highlight the contrast with the heavily mottled wall surface and the meticulously distressed frescoes.

In the master bath (opposite), my objective once again was to mimic the look of a rescued and reconstituted room built centuries ago. Here, next to the wooden beams, what appears to be repaired plaster and the

remains of a once glorious fresco are juxtaposed with contemporary pure white Thassos marble to underscore the clash of old and new. In both houses, the bathrooms and kitchens are meant to be read as contemporary additions to the aged structures. Trying to masquerade their modern functionality and fabrication would only be an invitation to kitsch.

DOORS AND DOORWAYS

Doorways naturally set the tone for the style and experience of a home. At the Outlook, rustic doors of weathered railroad ties open from the street into a Moroccan-style alcove that leads to the front garden (below, left). The entry to the house proper is framed with an assemblage of stone blocks and hand-shaped tiles, fitted together to create a complementary surround for a seventeenth-century studded iron door (left and opposite). In the Villa's living room, a formerly low, unremarkable passageway to an adjoining sitting area was enlarged and ennobled with a classical pediment (below). Like windows, portals such as these define the character of the home.

FLOORS

The floor of the master bedroom at the Villa (pages 84 and 85) was made from rift-sawn white oak laid in a chevron pattern—a style more common to France than Italy. The edges of every board were slightly beveled, and during installation I used an old credit card to create a slender gap between the boards, as if age and wear had caused the wood to shrink. The completed floor was then finished with a blended beeswax polish, which gave it a pleasing honey color. On a stair landing in the foyer near the bedroom, the plain wood floor was painted in a trompe l'oeil pattern suggesting inlaid marble (right, below).

At the Outlook, large slabs of thick sandstone, selected for their crude character, were cut into square tiles of different dimensions depending on the scale of the room. The edges of the tiles were hand-chipped and ground down to imitate centuries of wear and breakage, and then laid tightly together with no mortar between the pieces (right, above). Some of the tiles were intentionally cracked. In the Moroccan courtyard (opposite), handmade glazed bejmat tiles were laid in a chevron pattern with no mortar, adding a jolt of color and pattern to the garden setting. Unlike other areas of the house in which the palette is deliberately restrained, the bright tiles conspire with the yellow lemon trees and shocking pink bougainvillea to create a chromatic wonderland.

RUSTICATED
SURFACES

Over the years, I've pursued various techniques and materials to simulate aging and wear, many of which are surprisingly simple. Reclaimed railroad ties have been a reliable tool in that quest. After years of submersion in the earth, their crusty surfaces make a wonderful facing material. By being cut into one-inch-thick boards, they can be applied to walls, doors, gates, and even planter boxes.

A watery mixture of cement and white paint, applied with a brush, makes a very effective finish for virtually any object—like the giant ceramic pot at the Outlook (left, below), which looks as if it might be an antique vessel. Stone walkways can be lightly "soiled" with just about anything, including highly diluted paints and stains or even the leftover morning coffee, which I regularly splashed on the garden paths and stonework at the Villa.

WINDOWS

Architecturally, there is little else in a traditional house (or indeed a modern one) more important than its windows. They say everything about its quality. As a general rule, windows should have the thinnest possible muntins, rails, and stiles. When possible, I try to set windows into thick walls, which allow for deeply recessed reveals. At the Outlook, I set round windows with chamfered reveals into triple-framed walls to suggest the weight of antiquity. I also installed metal-framed French doors and windows in the library (overleaf). At the Villa, soaring, arched, Palladian-style windows set with panes of wavy salvaged glass (below) enhance the architectural forces of the living room.

TEXTILES AT THE VILLA

Textiles offer great opportunities for creative freedom. From precious vintage fragments to inexpensive contemporary prints, the mix can include anything that feels right. At the Villa, the canopy bed (left) is hung with panels cut from the embroidered covering of an eighteenth-century Indian howdah (the seat for riding elephants). In the library, an ottoman fashioned from a Persian textile and a scarred, cracked scrap of seventeenth-century leather is trimmed with brass nail heads (below, left). The library walls are covered in a distinctly traditional green damask (below and opposite) that serves as a foil to the more exotic textiles and artworks featured in the deliberately intimate room.

TEXTILES AT THE OUTLOOK

At the Outlook, variously patterned pieces of blue-and-white cloth—some French and others of undetermined origin—were combined to make a one-of-a-kind daybed (opposite). Outside, on the oceanfront terrace, a whitewashed bench is casually adorned with inexpensive cotton pillows from thrift shops and discount home furnishing emporiums (left). When it comes to fabric, one can abandon caution with the knowledge that, within limits, it's hard to go too far astray.

CEILINGS

Ceilings can take many forms, and efforts should be made to avoid succumbing to the usual lick of white paint. Beams, coffers, and cornice moldings, whether structural or cosmetic, can all be effective chapeaux for a room. In the library at the Outlook, the seemingly structural, gnarled seventeenth-century beams from Provence were affixed below the actual construction of the ceiling (opposite). For a bit of extra character, I hand-painted a pale blue chevron design in the spaces between the beams. The ceilings of the entry, living room, and master bedroom at the Outlook (right and below) feature closely spaced structural beams, in the Venetian style. I used the same technique for the dining room ceiling at the Villa (overleaf).

The foyer at the Villa, which showcases two of my paintings on the upper landing, retains its original 1920s mahogany coffered ceiling (overleaf). I hand-painted the housings of the recessed light fixtures to match the old stenciled panels in order to disguise the modern intervention. The bedroom's deep octagonal soffit (pages 84 and 85) is entirely new, but I designed its paneling and molding details to give it heft and presence, so that it does not announce itself as a conspicuous contemporary embellishment.

SCREENING

A thorough visual screening of the property is vital for the creation of one's own private and insulated world—if that is indeed your aim. At the Villa, a formal thirty-foot-high hedge of Ficus Nitida shields the house from the street (left), and a dense combination of trees, tall bamboo, walls, and vines (opposite) creates a visually impenetrable membrane that allows no hint of what might lie beyond.

The poet Robert Frost wrote that "good fences make good neighbors." I couldn't agree more. The Villa is flanked by neighboring properties a short distance away, but the invisibility I worked so hard to achieve endows my home with the semblance of a much grander estate than the square footage might suggest. Within the property, the outer world disappears, and you're left to enjoy whatever fantasy of domestic bliss you've conjured.

COLLECTIONS AND DISPLAY

Groupings of similar objects appear throughout both the Villa and the Outlook. In addition to the great pleasure I get from amassing these collections, they add immeasurably to the notion that their surroundings are continuing to evolve and grow, and are not merely snapshots frozen in time. In Malibu, a collection of sixteenth-century Syrian tiles, discovered in shards and now carefully repaired, lines the wall of a diminutive powder room (opposite).

At the Villa, in the main stairwell landing, a cardboard wall sculpture by Florian Baudrexel was commissioned for the space (pages 268 and 269). In the living room, a George III console is adorned with an array of antique stone heads (overleaf) that ranges from the Hellenistic period to sixteenth-century Italian to French Gothic. In the library, a group of African heads and masks is clustered on a seventeenth-century Italian table (pages 72 and 73).

Throughout the house, various artworks—ranging from a wooden fourteenth-century bishop (left) to a late Roman fragment depicting Venus to a 1985 welded steel sculpture by Anthony Caro (pages 40 and 41)—are displayed on pedestals of raw, knotty pine, a technique I borrowed from an admired European collector. The juxtaposition of the humble, unpretentious platforms and the precious works they support makes a striking statement.

ACKNOWLEDGMENTS

I am very grateful both to those directly responsible for this book and to those who have been so instrumental in helping me create the homes presented herein.

Much gratitude goes to my early champions Mayer Rus, for his tireless and invaluable guidance, and Mallery Roberts Morgan, for her unwavering support and editing prowess. Thank you to Jason Schmidt for his stunning photography, and to Mary Shanahan for the book's magnificent design.

Much gratitude to Margaret Russell and Michael Boodro, who have been wonderful boosters over the years. Thanks also to Charles Miers, Alexandra Tart, and Dung Ngo at Rizzoli.

Eternal gratitude to Marie Menefee and Missy Bernstein for their loyalty and their many years by my side at Studiolo. Thanks to those who have worked so hard with me in the gardens and contributed in so many other creative ways: Margarito Ruvalcaba, Edwin Almengor, and Glenn Fischer.

For her unbridled support and encouragement, my great love and thanks to Patricia Roach.

And lastly, to my late mother, Valery, who would have loved this.

First published in the United States of America in 2016
by Rizzoli International Publications, Inc.
300 Park Avenue South, New York, NY 10010
www.rizzoliusa.com

2016 2017 2018 2019 / 10 9 8 7 6 5 4 3 2 1

Distributed in the U.S. trade by Random House, New York .

Printed in China

ISBN-13: 978-0-8478-4740-2

Library of Congress Control Number: 2015953399

PHOTOGRAPH CREDITS
p. 196-197: © Tim Street-Porter/OTTO
p. 214: © Massimo Listri
p. 218: © Neville Morgan/Alamy
p. 219: *La Baie de Tanger vue de la Kasbah* © Jean-Pierre Loubat
p. 224: *Bab el Assa* © Jean-Pierre Loubat
p. 225: © David Burton/Alamy

*Half title page: Outside the Villa library, an alcove features an Italian giltwood console,
an Otto Piene painting, a late Roman bust, and lamps by Garouste and Bonetti.*

*Frontispiece: In the entry stairwell of the Villa, a target painting by Gary Lang hangs
above a first-century Roman torso.*

*Contents: A hemispheric niche clad in strategically eroded plaster creates an intimate
seating nook near the kitchen at the Outlook.*

*Endpapers: The branches of a precisely pruned one-hundred-year-old Pittosporum tree
in the Villa garden.*

DESIGNED BY MARY SHANAHAN